gifts
of
grace

MARY R. SCHRAMM

Discovering and Using Your Unique Abilities

gifts of grace

AUGSBURG Publishing House • Minneapolis

For John
who evokes my gifts
and gives me space to grow

To each is given the manifestation of the Spirit
for the common good (1 Cor. 12:7)

Contents

Preface

This is a book about discovering and using our gifts. It comes from my own struggle with discerning God's will for my life. Some years ago I read Elizabeth O'Connor's *Eighth Day of Creation,* and I began to see how my response to God's love for me was closely connected with using the talents and the Spirit gifts that are mine. This was a freeing concept for me and I am deeply appreciative of Elizabeth O'Connor for her excellent book.

During the past four years I have had the privilege of sharing with many groups the gospel message that each of us is chosen to be a special member of the body of Christ. Though we are each given grace-gifts, I am amazed at how ungifted people feel. It is my hope and prayer that as you read this you will be excited about being who you are and use your uniqueness to participate in a community of *shalom.*

A community of *shalom* is a community with a vision of wholeness. This beautiful Hebrew word is full of meaning. It was a way to say hello and a way to say good-bye. To say "is it *shalom* with you today?" meant, have you got enough money? *Shalom* includes health, prosperity, and well-being of every kind. It is important to understand however, that nowhere in the Old Testament does this word refer to inner tranquility or personal peace. According to biblical scholar Gerhard von Rad, "*Shalom* is not something concealed and inward. It manifests itself in a form of external well-being. *Shalom* is an emphatically social concept." When we expend our gifts for others we become a part of this biblical vision.

I want to thank Larry Rasmussen and my husband, John, for helping me avoid many theological pitfalls. I am especially grateful to my friend Tom Witt for his patience and many helpful suggestions as he read and reread my manuscript. My thanks also to David Martin for his sensitive illustrations and to the Holden Village community for giving me time and space to write.

Mary R. Schramm
Holden Village
Chelan, Washington 98816

1

Responding to God's Love

"What's there to do?" The question is a familiar one, and we expect it if we have children, especially as the summer months begin to be intolerably long, or when the television set is broken.

The question is not so appropriate when it comes from adults. We hesitate to ask, "What's there to do?" so we couch our concern and dissatisfaction in phrases that sound more "spiritual." We ask, "What is God's will for my life?" or "How can I respond to God's love?" Many of us feel scattered and uneasy. In our more honest moments we admit that God's silence is painful as we search for guidance.

Some of us will spend a lifetime waiting for that rare flash of insight that gives clarity to our struggle with vocation and discipleship. Others of us have the security of knowing the direction our lives should take in order to respond to God's love.

One of these people was a pastor visiting in our home some years ago. He felt a strong call upon his life to move into the center of a large East Coast city and work in an area known for its violence and poverty. In the pastor's denomination it was necessary for the regional conference of clergy to approve and financially support such a venture. When he stood up at the conference to describe what he wanted to do and to ask for the blessing of his colleagues, there was great alarm and disagreement. The discussion centered around the safety of the pastor's wife and children. Finally one clergyman said, "Not only will we *not* support this insane idea, we think you need psychological counseling! To take a family into that section of the city is ridiculous. If you cared at all for your family you would first consider their safety."

Our friend responded, "Where could my family and I be safer than in the very center of God's will for our lives?" His colleagues found it difficult to disagree with this truth, and he was given the financial support and affirmation he needed. The ministry was not easy and not always safe, but he found abundant life in living out God's will, in responding to God's love.

Our friend was fortunate. At that time in his life he and his family understood God's will for them and lived out that conviction. Many of us live tentatively as we wonder and worry about the direction our lives should take. We wait to be faithful disciples until we are certain of God's will, and one day we discover we are living "conditionally," for some future time. Conditional living is one of those subtle temptations that keeps us from fully living the moment and keeps us centered on self. We are robbed of joy that could be ours because "real" life is in the future.

Campus pastors tell us much of their time is spent counseling students who sincerely want to know God's will for their lives. Many of the volunteer staff who become part of the Holden Village community, where I live, say they want to spend time here to "get their heads together." They want help in discovering what it is God wants them to be and to do.

Michel Quoist, writing in *Meaning of Success*, asks:

Do you know what causes you the most suffering?

17

Your dissatisfaction, your unrest, your unresolved conflicts between what you want and what you actually have, what you would like to be and what you are, your hunger to know the mystery that is yourself and the mystery that is the world, . . . in a word, what causes you the most suffering is your failure to achieve fulfillment, your incompleteness.

We *do* suffer when we feel incomplete and unfulfilled. We discover that our life has little quality. It is hard to get up in the morning. The day does not seem like a gift to be celebrated but time to be endured. The routine of our day does not give us energy but leaves us feeling we are full of dead bones. Meaninglessness washes over us, leaving us wondering if God knows or cares how incomplete we feel. We sense we are part of the creation, waiting with eager longing to be set free from bondage (Rom. 8). The suffering of unfulfillment is evidence of our brokenness. Not only do we look around us and see symbols of alienation, we discover that even within ourselves the separation from God is real.

I am not a theologian or a psychologist, but a person who struggles with the sense of unrest Quoist writes about. My sense of unfulfillment comes more, perhaps, from my inability to respond to God's love for me. What is it God wants of me? It would be easier to get up in the morning if I had a sense of identity and ministry.

Quoist concludes his statement with the words, "Don't imagine for a moment that your deepest aspirations can be satisfied by something outside your-self." What is in the depths of ourselves that will satisfy our deepest need to feel fulfilled?

Through her writing, Elizabeth O'Connor has done a great service to the Christian community. Her book, *Eighth Day of Creation*, contains within it a profound, yet simple statement that helps to answer the question of Michel Quoist and the question of responding to God's love:

> We ask to know the will of God without guessing that his will is written into our very beings. We perceive that will when we discern our gifts. Our obedience and surrender to God are in a large part our obedience and surrender to our gifts. This is the message wrapped up in the parable of the talents. Our gifts are on loan. We are responsible for spending them in the world, and we will be held accountable.

This is good news! We are free to be the people God created us to be. Our response to God is intimately tied up with the talents and gifts that make us unique individuals. The "oughtness" that so often leaves us guilt-ridden is a heavy burden to carry. We cannot be the kind of person others think we should be, and, for that matter, we cannot even be the kind of person we ourselves would like to be. We are free to discover the uniqueness that is ours. Our "response-ability" is our ability to give back the gifts entrusted to us.

I assume I am writing to Christians who under-

stand that God's will for our lives is to follow Jesus.
I write under the assumption that Jesus is normative
for our life. It cannot be stated too strongly that for
the Christian, the use of our gifts is always for others
—for the common good. We are called to follow the
example of our Lord in self-giving love. We do this in
a physical way, by offering the gift of ourselves to
others.

St. Paul begs his readers to give God their very
bodies as an act of true worship:

> Therefore, my brothers, I implore you by God's
> mercy to offer your very selves to him: a living
> sacrifice, dedicated and fit for his acceptance, the
> worship offered by mind and heart. Adapt your-
> selves no longer to the pattern of this present world,
> but let your minds be remade and your whole na-
> ture thus transformed. Then you will be able to
> discern the will of God, and to know what is good,
> acceptable, and perfect (Rom. 12:1-2 NEB).

What does it mean to "offer your very selves" to
God or to "present your bodies as a living sacrifice,"
as the RSV says? It means we step forward with our
talents and our grace-gifts and ask to be used as we
are for accomplishing God's will. To come as we are,
unique and transformed by the Spirit working within
us, is to avoid letting the world squeeze us into a
mold. As an act of worship we celebrate who we are
and offer ourselves—with our limitations and our
strengths. We are equipped to be part of the body of
Christ. We put ourselves in the center of God's will

for our lives when we exercise our gifts on behalf of another.

In the *Lutheran Book of Worship* is a prayer in which we offer who we are as a response to God's love:

> We offer with joy and thanksgiving what you have first given us—our selves, our time, and our possessions, signs of your gracious love. Receive them for the sake of him who offered himself for us, Jesus Christ our Lord. Amen.

God's will for our life is that we learn to follow Jesus. God's will for our life is to discover our gifts and to be fully who we were created to be. These are not mutually exclusive statements. To follow Jesus is to be fully oneself. The gospel means we can be excited about being who we are, not wishing we were someone else.

From Carol Powers

2

Someone Creative Lives in My House

"Then God said, let us make man in our image, after our likeness" (Gen. 1:26). It is difficult to comprehend what it means to be created in the likeness of God. Because we have seen God revealed in Jesus, we know God is love, God is forgiving, and that God suffers. What we may fail to realize is that since God is a creator, we are also creators. Creativity is part of the essence of being human. Most of us deny this. When I have asked a group of people at the beginning of a discussion on gifts and creativity, how many consider themselves to be gifted, creative people, very few raise their hands. It cannot be that I speak to especially humble groups! People generally do not feel gifted. When I ask if they know any creative, gifted persons, most will respond with names of entertainers, artists, good preachers, or the choir soloist. The church has *not* done a good job liberating the gifts hiding within the body of Christ. We have devoted ourselves to explaining doctrines but have left a large group of unfulfilled, restless church members who have little sense of joy and celebration. They are never called upon to be creative, and they feel little or no responsibility for the ministry of their congregation.

"But grace was given to each of us according to the measure of Christ's gift. Therefore it is said, 'When he ascended on high he led a host of captives, and he gave gifts to men' " (Eph. 4:7-8). This has been paraphrased to read, "He triumphed over all the spiritual forces that might endanger our salvation, returning like a victor bearing spoils, which he distributes to his followers." Here we have a picture of a generous Savior, lavishly giving to each of us *charismata*—gifts of grace.

The parable of the talents (Matt. 25:14-30) is another reminder that we are all gifted people. A man of some wealth took a trip and entrusted to his servants all his capital. The man was aware that some of his servants were more responsible than others, so distribution of the talents was made on the ability of the servants to go out into the world and use them. The third servant who hid his talent in the ground is the disappointment in the story. He was guilty of sloth. (Sloth, Lewis Mumford points out, is one of the seven deadly sins our culture has not yet turned into a virtue.) The third servant let others worry about investing their talents while he allowed sloth and fear to dictate his actions. The servant's fear was his undoing. Knowing his master to be a shrewd businessman, he hid his talent. As we read the conclusion of the parable, we too sense the kind of hell that results from unfaithful, unfulfilled lives.

In her book *Centering* Mary Richards writes, "A creative being lives inside us, and we better get out of its way, for it will give us no peace until we do."

Carl Jung says much the same thing: "Vocation [our calling] acts like a law of God. The creative person is overpowered, captive . . . unless one assents to the power of the inner voice, the personality cannot evolve." We feel a sense of self-betrayal when we cannot or will not use our gifts, when we will not give way to that creative being living inside each of us.

The artist Richard Caemmerer is a man whose creative genius causes him to get out of bed at midnight and begin to paint. He cannot rest until the canvas is completed. The same is true for composer David Martin. The creative being inside David gives him very little rest. He tells me, "I feel possessed at times. I hear music going through my brain at night, and I get no sleep until I get up and put the notes down on paper."

Dorothy Day was creative in a different way. As she saw the plight of the poor and those for whom life was extremely hard, she created ways to help relieve their suffering. She put herself in the center of God's will by giving her life—her gifts and her talents—to work and live among these people.

Matthew Fox believes that "at the heart of creativity is seeing connections. This is how compassion begins." We become compassionate when we realize everything is connected—plants, animals and all people. When one part of God's creation is hurting, the rest of the creation suffers. To enrich the lives of others, or to enter into their suffering, we have only to give the creative being that lives in our house a chance to emerge.

3

But My Gifts
Are So Simple!

By now you may be saying, "But I'm not an artist or a composer or a Dorothy Day. I'm a candle—not a star."

In a culture where big, more and flashy are success words, we tend to view with some embarrassment our "insignificant" gifts. After all, doesn't a gift have to be outstanding before we share it with another?

Gifts cannot be ranked according to their worth. While we might agree that some people are called to larger tasks in the kingdom, God's grace is that we are all called to some work. The old Shaker folk song reminds us that even a simple gift is acceptable and that employing it will bring us joy because it will engage us in the "place just right"—the place where God wants us to be.

'Tis a gift to be simple, 'Tis a gift to be free.
'Tis a gift to come down where we ought to be,
And when we find ourselves in the place just right
'Twill be in the valley of love and delight.
When true simplicity is gained,
To bow and to bend we will not be ashamed.
To turn and to turn will be our delight,
Till by turning, turning we come 'round right.

We often share ourselves with another by way of a simple act of caring. If asked, we would never think to call it a gift. In *Out of Solitude* Henri Nouwen writes, "Real care excludes indifference and is the opposite of apathy. The word 'care' finds its roots in the Gothic 'Kara' which means lament. The basic meaning of care is to grieve, to experience sorrow, to cry out with." All of us were given the gift of *kara*. In some, the gift is more developed, in others the risk of caring is swallowed up by fear of being vulnerable. When we care deeply for another, we open ourselves up to the possibility of being hurt or of being known more than we care to be.

My mother lives in an apartment in Seattle. She shares a common laundry with 30 other tenants. One day, while doing her laundry, she noticed an elderly man across the room putting his coins in the dryer. He had obviously been crying. My mother went over to him and said, "I've seen you in the building, but I don't know your name." She introduced herself and then said, "I notice you are crying. Is there anything I can do for you?"

The man wiped his eyes with the back of his hand. "Thank you, but no," he said. As more tears started to come he looked at her and added. "Yes, there is something but I don't expect you'd want to do it. It is one year ago today that my wife died, and in all that time no one has put their arms around me and hugged me." With that my mother, Norwegian as she is, wrapped her arms around the stranger and both began to cry as they rocked in each other's arms.

When my mother told me this story later, she did so with great embarrassment. "I don't know what got into me," she exclaimed. "What if someone had come into the laundry room and seen me with my arms around a stranger! But somehow it just seemed the right thing to do."

It was the right thing to do. My mother has a gift.

She was willing to risk looking foolish by opening herself up to the need of a stranger.

On the teaching staff at Holden Village several years ago was a charming Protestant nun from Germany. Sister Ingeborg delighted us all with the story of a simple gift of sensitivity. As Sister Ingeborg explained the vow of poverty she had taken, she added that deep down she still had a desire for a certain white nightgown with pink lace she had once seen. One day in the mail came a package from her mother, and in it was the lacy nightgown. Happily she showed the gown to the other sisters and to the Mother Superior. "Yes, it is lovely, Sister," Mother said, "but do you *need* it?"

"Of course I didn't need it," Sister Ingeborg told us. "I already had one nightgown, and you can't wear two." Seeing her disappointed face, an older sister leaned across the table and said, "Sister Ingeborg, my nightgown is all worn out. Do you think I could have your *old* gown?"

As she related this story, Sister Ingeborg's eyes still showed her joy at being the recipient of a gift of sensitivity. Of course the older sister could have her gown! The sensitivity of the other nun, who expressed her gift in a caring act, will never be forgotten by Sister Ingeborg.

We tend to smile and say, "Nice story, but God certainly has bigger work to be done than that simple act of gift-giving. There are too many hurts and problems facing us to spend time being sensitive to the disappointment of a nun over a lacy nightgown!"

Wrong! That kind of conclusion again leads to the "conditional living" trap. We may use our lofty preoccupation with the larger problems of the world as reason for neglecting the hurting people around us. We fail to take a hot meal to the shut-in down the street because we are too busy raising consciousness about, or raising funds for, world hunger. It is easier to feel compassion for a starving child looking at us from a page of *Time* magazine than to love the neighbor's kid with a runny nose who disrupts our day looking for attention. I dream of some day being part of an inclusive community farm. The farm would include elderly and terminally ill residents, and yet I cannot show the necessary compassion to live comfortably with a senile mother-in-law right now.

The Bell Telephone ads tell us to reach out and touch someone. So does the gospel. If we are a candle, we will touch one or two people at a time. The light of a star touches more lives, but both are authentic gifts, illuminating dark places.

I felt like a candle in Washington, D.C., when I discovered one of our garbage collectors didn't know how to read. His name was Michael, and since I was eager to try out my newly acquired Laubach literacy skills, I offered to teach him how. For a year Michael came once a week to our home, where together we struggled to make him literate. I never was able to teach him to read, but I will never forget the last night he came for a lesson. I walked out with him to the alley where he had parked his truck.

He had brought a large watermelon as a gift. As we perched on the back of the truck eating a piece of melon, he said rather shyly, "I'm awfully sorry I couldn't learn to read, but it was good to make a friend." I could have hugged him—and I did.

Meister Eckhart, a 14th-century mystic and theologian, preached to his congregation, "It often happens that what seems trivial to us is more important to God than we think important . . . . we ought simply to follow where God leads—that is, to do what we are most inclined to do, to go where we are repeatedly admonished to go—to where we feel most drawn. If we do that, God gives us his greatest in our least and never fails."

4

No One Asks Me
Who I Am

Some of my most unpleasant memories of church are of those reluctant Christian education teachers who disliked what they were doing. I could sense even at a very young age which teachers could hardly wait for the hour to be over. Not even the best educational helps the church could provide erased the fact that the teacher was there out of "oughtness."

Many of us have had the experience of joining a new congregation and never being asked how we perceive ourselves, what we would like to become involved in, or what interests us. Instead we are thrust into a round hole, even though we are a square peg. The congregation needs Sunday school teachers, choir members, someone to serve meals-on-wheels, and a member for the stewardship committee. Pick one. Now we must add to all our other guilty burdens the feeling that we really ought to plug in somewhere, so perhaps we had better volunteer to teach Sunday school.

Gordon Cosby at the Church of the Savior in Washington, D.C., is a pastor who understands how important it is for Christians to help one another discover who they are and to help them use their gifts. The vitality and strength of that congregation witnesses to the truth that when gifts are evoked, the church comes into being. Churches fail, Gordon Cosby says, because we bring people into the fellowship and try to make them into something they are not. This is a sad perversion of the gospel. To evoke the gifts of individuals is to acknowledge and affirm the work of God in them.

34

It is a great temptation to cling to cherished dreams of how a church program should look. We assign individuals to the evangelism committee who may not have the gift of communicating formally or informally with strangers. As a result they sense inner terror—and not joy—at sharing their faith. The woman dragged into a leadership role of the women's group will feel resentment instead of joy. She says by her attitude, "Someone had to do this, and no one else would, so I'm stuck!"

Recently I was asked to share leadership responsibility for a congregational retreat. Part of the retreat time was to be spent reexamining the structure and constitution of the congregation. Committees and boards had been developed to replace the council structure. The idea was excellent because many more members would be involved in leadership and decision making. As the retreat progressed, however, it was obvious that little or no thought had been given to first discovering the interests and the talents of the members. Assignments to the various boards would be made, but no process had been designed to help in discerning individual gifts.

I can remember a time in our parish when we had no Christian education because no one felt their gfit was teaching. This was not unfaithful nor were we uncomfortable with the prospect that for a time there would be no classes. The parents of the children began to take a deeper interest and came up with a creative solution. They teamed up and taught the children themselves, agreeing that training in the

Christian life was also a parental role. The teaching carried over into the devotional life of the families, and deeper relationships between parents and the children developed.

Let me add a disclaimer. Any who have been involved in a congregation know we can't always dispense with Sunday school or the various chores and maintenance tasks that need to be done if congregaticnal life is to run smoothly. It is naive to claim everyone should be doing only those things that engage them exclusively in the use of their talents and gifts. At times, for the sake of the proper functioning of the body of Christ, we may be assigned a task by the rest of the community. We may be asked to develop a gift or to perform a function to strengthen the fellowship. It would be dangerous to limit the work of God's Spirit to one avenue of "call" or one understanding of how gifts are evoked.

Some jobs may not appear to us to be very creative. However, in a congregation, as in any family, things need to be done that are not especially enjoyable for us. This is why community is so important. It is simply more fun to share tedious jobs with a group of people. Dish teams at Holden Village provide little opportunity for creativity, but taking a turn and sharing a job with seven others makes doing dishes not only tolerable, but provides a good hour of fellowship.

When working with others, we may also discover that a tedious job for us is the task that best uses the gift of another. Let's use Paul's image of the body in

1 Corinthians 12. If you, as the left arm of the body, begin to feel resentment at having to do the job of both arms, then look around and see if the right arm is hanging limply, waiting to be involved. For the freedom of each arm, both need to be exercised. Unexercised muscles atrophy, leaving a weak and useless member. Both arms working together will free up more time for doing the kind of ministry that makes the best use of our uniqueness.

There is something more to be said about redeeming the time spent on less creative jobs. A friend who worked on an auto assembly line in Detroit said he learned about praying from studying the lives of the saints. He remembered that Brother Lawrence practiced the presence of God at all times. This monastery cook, who spent a lifetime working among pots and pans, wrote, "Likewise in the business of the kitchen (to which I have naturally a great aversion), having accustomed myself to do everything there for the love of God, and with prayer upon all occasions for grace to do his work well, I have found everything easy during the fifteen years I have been employed there."

I remember asking our housepainter if he enjoyed his work. "Not always," he replied, "but I have become so skilled at what I do, I can spend much of my day in prayer." Our housepainter had discovered a way to have a sabbath time in each day. Like Brother Lawrence, he felt "more united to God in his ordinary occupations, than when he left them for devotion in retirement."

Finding creative ways to live in all circumstances and knowing that we are to live with a servant's mind (even being willing to do those things that are not always fulfilling and enjoyable for us) does not deny the premise of discovering our uniqueness. If the Spirit provides the gifts necessary for the body of Christ to function, why aren't we more serious about discovering these gifts? Part of the gospel message for each individual is, "As part of the body, you are needed. Let us help you discover your uniqueness and use your gifts in ministry." When this is done, some of the "normal church activities" may not happen, but the potential for a great variety of service, where people are genuinely excited about ministry, will enliven and enrich not only the body but those whose lives we daily touch.

5

We Need One Another
to Discover Our Gifts

As we look around the group of people we call our Christian community, we sometimes wonder how such a combination of individuals can ever be called "the body of Christ." And yet there is something salutary about being stuck with each other. We would never have chosen these persons to form our God-family, and so we need to look beyond superficialities and probe the mystery that makes us one functioning organism. Together we form a "conspiracy"—a group of people who "breathe together" for a common purpose. Our *unity*, however, is not to be confused with *uniformity*.

The apostle Paul speaks strongly about our unity:

> For just as the body is one and has many members, and all the members of the body, though many, are one body, so it is with Christ. For by one Spirit we were all baptized into one body—Jews or Greeks, slaves or free—and all were made to drink of one Spirit (1 Cor. 12:12-13).

One body, one Spirit. This is the unity holding us together. The unity of our God-family reflects itself in the shared joys and sorrows of the members making up the body. In the Jewish families of Paul's time, one child in trouble reflected upon the entire family. The joy of one member was shared by the family as if that joy were theirs. This same sense of oneness is felt when the church is functioning as a healthy body.

This unity in Christ does not mean we must all be alike. Thank God there is no one else just like me—

40

or you! How dull and narrow our experiences would be. It pleased God to create infinite varieties of gifts in a multitude of combinations. To envy another is to belittle the person you are. God's creation (including each of us) is precious to God, and to despise the creation is to heap contempt on its Creator.

Several years ago at Holden Village, a young staff woman named Beth came to me, upset because she felt inadequate. She expressed anger at not being able to understand many of the discussions of theology or literature that take place in the community. She was not able to articulate her feelings in a group.

"I am so stupid!" she wailed. "Why did God make me the way I am?" No amount of talk could convince her she too was gifted in a variety of ways. It took an understanding member of the community to help this young woman realize that her gifts were just as important to the community as the gifts of knowledge and articulation. It happened in this way.

One evening the worship service was based on 1 Corinthians 12—Paul's discussion of the individual members making up the body of Christ. Charles, who was in charge of the worship, asked Beth to participate. Her immediate response was, "I can't; I don't speak well."

"You don't have to say anything," Charles assured her. "Your role will be entirely nonverbal. You are to create a body by borrowing different parts from the members of the community."

And so Beth did. With Charles crouched down behind a small table, she pretended to take from one person a head, which she carefully pretended to place on the table. Immediately Charles' head appeared above the table top. Next a torso pretended to be placed under Charles' head, followed by two different arms and legs from other individuals attending the service. By this time Charles had swung his legs over the table and was sitting there, all the time complaining that he disliked the size of his shoulders given to him; he hated wearing glasses; one arm was too short; and his left leg too hairy. This much of the drama had been planned. As Beth stood there listening to his complaints, she began to reverse her actions. Quietly she pretended to remove one leg and return it to its owner. Then the other leg and the arms. As she did this, Charles quickly changed his chatter. "Oh, that's OK," he said, "don't take my arms. I'll try to make the best of them. No, no! Leave my torso. I can probably do something with the narrow shoulders—wear shoulder pads perhaps." The last we heard from him, as his head disappeared under the table, was something about not really being all that happy with what he had been given anyway.

This creative drama spoke to all of us and especially to Beth. "I see what you've been trying to tell me," she said to me later. "Help me find my place in this community. What can I give that is my gift to share?" Beth had a gift of humor and a servant's mind. It was part of our responsibility as a community to help her recognize these gifts as essential to our life together.

On my desk I later found a Martin Buber quote Beth had paraphrased. "Every person born into this world represents something new, something that never existed before, something original and unique. It is my duty . . . to know that there has never been anyone like Beth in the world, for if there had been . . . there would have been no need for Beth in the world. Every single person is a new thing in the world and is called upon to fulfill a particularity in this world."

Stars and candles—there is room for both. Both give joy. Both are beautiful. Both give light in dark places.

In 1 Corinthians 7:7 Paul wrote, "I wish you were all like I myself am. But each has his own special gift from God, one of one kind and one of another." So often we spend time wishing we were someone else instead of being excited about the person we are. We also waste energy by remaking others in our image instead of affirming who *they* are. Any performer is quick to admit that the more appreciative the audience, the better the performance. Genuine appreciation is soul food. To say "you can do it!" is a way of conveying the gospel message, because we see in the other a worthwhile person—one in whom the spirit of God lives and one for whom Christ died.

We need one another if gifts are to be evoked. Every Christian community would do well to remember Bob Dylan's words, "one who is not busy bein' born is busy dyin'." We can help keep people from dyin' by helping them with this birthing process— helping them discover the creative, gifted being bubbling up inside, waiting to be developed. Each day, as we discover our continuing uniqueness, we discover we are being born again and again and again.

Writing at age 82, Florida Scott-Maxwell confesses one would think that when you are in your 80s you could get by with being whatever you wanted to be. After all, don't people forgive anything if one is old? Not so! If we are eight or 80, we are responsible for helping one another discover and use the result of Spirit-work in our lives.

There is another role the community must play, and this is perhaps more difficult for us. Along with genuine *affirmation*, there are times for *confrontation*. There is great pain when we do not speak the truth in love, and there is also some pain when it *is* spoken in love. Confrontation in the Christian community is not a way of getting rid of an irritant or one with whom we may differ. The purpose of confrontation is to strengthen the relationships within the body. Small problems grow rapidly and soon lose all proportion if we are never willing to be confrontive.

There was a member of the Holden community who considered her gift to be counseling. After several staff had been hurt through her counseling, it became necessary to discuss with the counselor her role in the community. It was difficult to say to her, "We do not see your gift as one of giving counsel. You are not strengthening the body by assuming this role; in fact, you weaken it." Because there was a deep level of trust, this could be done. It is not enough to say to another, "That is not your gift." It is also important to help the other find the gift that *is* theirs. This trust level is developed when small groups of people are willing to be vulnerable and celebrate together strengths and weaknesses—people who commit themselves to each other to meet regularly for prayer and conversation and study of the Scriptures. These are people who also work together, play and party together. The frequent touching of one another's lives creates the fertile soil that allows growth because of acceptance and trust. In a large congregation it would seem impossible to sense this kind of healing community unless great care is taken to develop a milieu where people learn to know one another.

A community of people helping each other to evoke their gifts will find little time for jealousy, envy, or standing in judgment. Each person—black, yellow, white, brown, male or female—is an image of God and gives God great joy. All need to be incorporated into the body, nourished and given concern. Without this inclusive care, the body is not complete and does not function properly. St. Paul wrote eloquently about the members of the body being equal in their importance. Should an ear be upset because it is not an eye or the eye say it has no need of the hand? Wishing we had a particular gift because we see it in another is to avoid using the gifts *we* have been given.

The Hebrew word for Satan means *hinderer*. It is demonic to hinder others from discovering their full potential or standing in the way as they attempt to exercise their gifts because we are prejudiced or envious. Ann Herbert has a delightful parable about the problem of envy:

In the beginning God didn't make just one or two people; he made a bunch of us. Because he wanted us to have a lot of fun and he said you can't really have fun unless there's a whole gang of you. So he put us all in this sort of playground park place called Eden and told us to enjoy.

At first we did have fun just like he expected. We played all the time. We rolled down the hills, waded in the streams, climbed the trees, swung on the vines, ran in the meadows, frolicked in the woods, hid in the forest, and acted silly. We laughed a lot.

Then one day this snake told us that we weren't having real fun because we weren't keeping score. Back then, we didn't know what score was. When he explained it, we still couldn't see the fun. But he said that we should give an apple to the person who was best at playing and we'd never know who was best unless we kept score. We could all see the fun of that. We were all sure we were best.

It was different after that. We yelled a lot. We had to make up new scoring rules for most of the games we played. Other games, like frolicking, we stopped playing because they were too hard to score. By the time God found out about our new fun, we were spending about forty-five minutes a day in actual playing and the rest of the time working out the score. God was wroth about that—very, very wroth.

He said we couldn't use his garden anymore because we weren't having any fun. We said we were having lots of fun and we were. He shouldn't have got upset just because it wasn't exactly the kind of fun he had in mind.

He wouldn't listen. He kicked us out and said we couldn't come back until we stopped keeping score. To rub it in (to get our attention, he said), he told us we were all going to die anyway and our scores wouldn't mean anything.

He was wrong. My cumulative all-game score is now 16,548 and that means a lot to me. If I can raise it to 20,000 before I die I'll know I've accomplished something. Even if I can't my life has a great deal of meaning because I've taught my children to score high and they'll all be able to reach 20,000 or even 30,000 I know.

Really, it was life in Eden that didn't mean anything. Fun is great in its place, but without scoring there's no reason for it. God has a very superficial view of life and I'm glad my children are being raised away from his influence. We were lucky to get out. We're all very grateful to the snake.

Keeping score has everything to do with competition and nothing whatever to do with compassion. Compassion is that gift that allows us to view another with a love that forgets self and finds us willing to share our lives in deep respect for another as a member of the body. To be compassionate means we must stop judging others. Henri Nouwen writes in *Way of the Heart,* "In order to be of service to others, we have to die to them. . . . To die to our neighbor means to stop judging them, to stop evaluating them, and thus to become free to be compassionate. Compassion can never coexist with judgment because judgment creates the distance, the distinction, which prevents us from really being with the other."

A compassionate community of Christ will not be worrying about being an eye or an ear or a little toe. The community will not be judging or envious, but will earnestly seek to discover the gifts of each member. This is one of the ways we love one another.

6

Room to Be and to Grow

A gift we can give one another in Christian community is the *space* for each member to grow. The word *salvation* has the Hebrew concept of wide spaces. The stem of the verb *save* means roomy, broad areas—the opposite of the feeling that one is constricted, choked, or hemmed in. The social concept of salvation impiles giving space and a sense of freedom to those who are boxed in or enslaved. For a person to be whole and creative, space and freedom from rigidity are essential.

Alan McGinnis, writing in *Friendship Factor* says:

> One of the dangers of being a psychologist/reformer is that you are tempted to remake people in your own image. But God made each unique and there is vast mystery and beauty surrounding the human soul. Good psychologists are like good astronomers who spend their lives studying the stars to determine why certain stellar systems behave as they do and why black holes exist. And in the end they are even more in awe of the grandeur of it all. . . . If I can help my patients understand who God made them to be and help them be that person, it is quite enough.

During an airplane flight I was reading an interesting magazine article. A wealthy family had decided to give large amounts of money to each of fifty individuals throughout the United States who showed promise of developing their unique gifts. Budding artists, scientists, philosophers, inventors, and those in other fields would be given this free gift of money to enable them to devote time and energy to their work. There were to be no strings attached. No accounting was to be made as to how the money was spent or if the venture was successful. (The article ended with, "Don't call us, we'll call you!")

This kind of trust level and ability to give one another space is important in community. I do not mean to say that accountability is not important, but we dare not expect everyone to conform to our idea of what Christians should be or how they should live out a Christian life.

The following story has been around for a long time, and I regret I do not know the author to give the proper credit. It expresses the tragedy and waste when structures and individuals do not allow room for growth and developing creativity.

Once a little boy went to school. It was quite a big school, but when the boy found he could go right to his room from the playground outside he was happy, and the school didn't seem quite so big anymore. One morning when the little boy had been in school for awhile, the teacher said, "Today we are going to make a picture."

"Good," thought the little boy. He liked to make pictures. He could make lions and tigers and trains and boats. He took out his crayons and began to draw. But the teacher said, "Wait. It's not time to begin." And she waited until everyone looked ready. "Now," said the teacher, "we are going to make flowers."

"Good," thought the little boy, and he began to make beautiful flowers with his orange and pink and blue crayons. But the teacher said, "Wait." She drew a picture on the blackboard. It was red with a green stem. "There, now you may begin."

The little boy looked at the teacher's flower. He liked his better, but he did not say this. He just turned his paper over and made a flower like the teacher's. It was red with a green stem.

On another day the teacher said, "Today we are going to make something with clay." "Good," thought the little boy. He could make all kinds of things with clay—snakes and snowmen and elephants and mice—and he began to pinch and pull his ball of clay. But again the teacher said, "Wait. I will show you how." And she showed everyone how to make one deep dish. The little boy just rolled his clay into a round ball and made a dish like the teacher's. And pretty soon the little boy learned to wait and to watch and to make things just like the teacher's. And pretty soon he didn't make things of his own anymore.

And then it happened that the little boy and his family moved to another city and the boy had to go to another school. On the very first day he went to school the teacher said, "Today we are going to make a picture." "Good," thought the boy and he waited for the teacher to tell him what to do. But the teacher didn't say anything. She just walked around the room. When she came to the boy she said, "Don't you want to make a picture?"

"Yes," said the boy. "What are we going to make?"

"Well, I don't know until you make it," said the teacher.

"How should I make it?" said the boy.

"Why, any way you like!"

"And any color?"

"Any color," said the teacher. "If everyone made the same thing in the same color, how would I know who made what and which was which?"

"I don't know," said the boy, and he began to draw a flower. It was red with a green stem.

7

Discovering Our Worth
in Times of Solitude

Discerning our gifts takes a community of people to support us, confront us, and to give us space to grow. Discerning our gifts also takes time alone. For the Christian, times of solitude and prayer are as essential to life as breathing. "Don't just do something, stand there!" is very good advice. The stilling of our spirits is possible only after we quiet our bodies and still our minds. God knew that for our total health, six days of work was enough. The sabbath was a gift to us. The sabbath was grace. Each of our days also needs a sabbath time.

Earlier I mentioned that a friend on the auto assembly line and our housepainter had found sabbath times while they worked. Both of these men felt that at the present time they could not change jobs. They found a deep measure of freedom because they accepted what they could not change and within that situation used their time creatively. Those of us whose daily activities do not allow us to meditate, need to set aside time to create that distance from normal activity where we can listen to the Spirit trying to get our attention.

Even when we desire to set aside a sabbath in our day, we find it difficult to find the time. We may feel indispensable to whatever activity we are engaged in, or perhaps we have a hard time learning to say "no" to the demands put upon us by friends, employer, family, or our own ego.

Spending time alone is not always popular—in fact, some would consider it to be socially unacceptable. We are judged favorably by our activity, not our quiet, inconspicuous moments. James Carroll bemoans the fact that he cannot go fishing without a pole. If you sit on the river's edge without a pole, someone might come and haul you away, or at least assume you are on public welfare!

But it is unfair to place on others the entire blame for our reluctance to spend time in solitude. Solitude is often painful for us. While it is difficult to be honest with others, it is more difficult to be honest with ourselves. We would rather hide in our busy-ness than face ourselves in quiet times. If our prayers are not moments of honesty—or at least begin that way—they do not open us up to God, and we end up talking with ourselves. God is waiting to speak to us, but we do not hear because we are surrounded by the noise of our own agenda. We do not see without illusions, because we are unwilling to take off our blindfolds. Not wanting to be seen, we refuse to take off our masks.

We need time alone if we are going to do some serious reflection on who we are and the gifts we have. Paul writing in Romans 12 asks us not to think of ourselves more highly than we ought to think, but asks us to think with sober judgment. This requires unmasking and dis-illusioning. Just as we need the mirror of community to give us a reflection of ourselves and our gifts, so we need the mirror of solitude. Honest evaluation and introspection come during quiet times of prayer and meditation.

Solitude is also important to us because it is here that we begin to understand that we are acceptable people, not because we are successful, good, or beautiful, but because the One who loves us has called us to be an essential part of the body of Christ.

Many of us grew up with the idea that our worth as individuals is equated with our successes or how busy we appear to be. Our self-esteem is so closely linked to the success or failure of everything we do that we begin to judge ourselves by what others think of us. Henri Nouwen calls this being in the world and also *of* the world, because we have sold our identity to the judges of this world. In solitude we discover this success-mentality is a false illusion. In his book *Out of Solitude* Nouwen says:

> A life without a lonely place, that is, a life without a quiet center, easily becomes destructive. When we cling to the results of our actions as our only way of self-identification, then we become possessive and defensive and tend to look at our fellow human beings more as enemies to be kept at a distance than as friends with whom we share the gift of life.

I plead guilty to judging people often by "the results of their actions." On a recent retreat I asked a woman what she did. She laughed and put her arm around me as she replied, "I'm just a full-time person." She gave me a good answer. This woman knew the difference between being and doing, between who she was and what she did.

At the next party when you have been introduced to someone, ask them who they are instead of what they do. Their responses will give strong clues as to their self-identification and self-worth. "I'm a mother." "I'm a professor." "I'm a widow." "I have a hearing problem." "I'm a failure in the eyes of my folks." I often think of a man living near our farm in West Virginia. He is known as "the other Harris." Is one to assume there is a Mr. Harris of more importance than this man whose first name no one seems to know?

Many of us suffer from a low self-image. We consider ourselves to be worthwhile only in relation to our successes and the approval of others. In Christian community we should find the words of encouragement that we are special, gifted individuals. In times of solitude and prayer we find even more assurance that we are worthwhile, redeemed, Spirit-graced children of God.

8

The Spirit Says, "Enjoy, Enjoy!"

A Greek neighbor used to lean over our mutual fence and say to me in her broken English, "Enjoy, enjoy!" She would close her eyes and tilt her head back to feel the sun on her face. She also said these words when she pointed to her amazing fig tree, sprawling in the corner of her yard where the fence met the house. She said, "Enjoy, enjoy!" when she would hand us a plate of *moussaka* she had made for our dinner. Mrs. Loukas enjoyed life as a gift. She delighted in racing around her small backyard with her mongrel dog, so overfed that it was barely able to keep its belly from dragging on the sidewalk. The dog always seemed grateful when the romp was over and he could flop down in the shade under the back steps. Mrs. Loukas would laugh and try to coax and tease her pet out into the sunshine with words I did not understand.

Our family adopted the neighbor's phrase. It became the words that accompanied a gift and was even the way we began to say good-bye to one another in the morning. It was shorthand for "Have a good day. Enjoy what you will be doing."

Enjoyment of a task, though not the only criterion, is a clue to identifying the gifts that were given to us. The gifts God gave were not meant to inflict pain or rob us of life, but to give *abundant* life. Jesus said, "I am the door; if any one enters by me, he will be saved, and will go in and out and find pasture. The thief comes only to steal and kill and destroy; I came that they may have life, and have it abundantly" (John 10:9-10).

The abundant life Jesus promises is not the over-stuffed feeling we have following many meals. Abundance is not the accumulation of material goods, which, according to the media, promises to eliminate dissatisfaction, boredom, and emptiness. We have abundant life when we experience the genuine wealth of living within God's will for our lives. There is joy in the abundant life because we find ourselves living at a higher level of self-giving love. In the metaphor Jesus used, the sheep have joy and peace, not because they are cozied up inside the sheepfold, but because they can *go in and out,* knowing they are within the care of the shepherd. The context of abundant life is seen in freedom from fear and in the security of knowing that nothing can separate the sheep from the shepherd's love.

Abundant life includes the struggles, the confrontations that give us pain, the losses we endure, as well as the more obvious blessings of friends, work to do, or a warm bed at night. We know joy when we choose to live with the awareness of God's presence in *all* we experience.

Enjoy, enjoy! Somehow we in the church have the mistaken idea that following Jesus and the way of the cross means a joyless existence. If it doesn't hurt, it must not be worthwhile, we surmise. "What's wrong with me?" someone will ask. "I'm so happy in my job it makes me wonder if this is what God intends for me to be doing." Or someone else confesses, "I can hardly wait for the weekend to come. The volunteer time I'm giving fills me with a greater sense of joy than my daily job."

Both of these statements point out something about the joy of exercising our gifts. If using our gifts and sensing fulfillment and peace is associated with our work-week, we can thank God. Many people find the best use of their gifts does not coincide with how they earn their paycheck. The sense of unfulfillment, caused by that creative being inside us, needs attention, and perhaps it is after the nine-to-five routine that the unrest is quieted. It may be in our leisure hours that we engage in the kind of ministry where we feel free to express our gifts.

Enjoying who you are and what you are doing is the best witness to our Lord. This does not mean that when we use our gifts we will always be able to say we are happy or having fun, but the joy, the enjoyment, will be obvious. There is no one more depressing to be around than a fanatical, humorless Christian. No wonder the church grows so slowly when the witness we speak is hardly heard (and frequently ignored) because it comes from the mouths of those whose joyless lives do not match their proclamation. We can speak the good news of the gospel, but if *we* are not good news, our witness is shallow. Few pay attention to the Christian message if it is not embodied in lives that radiate joy (not a plastic Christian smile, but real joy!). It is easy to distinguish these people from those enduring a life filled with oughtness. To perform a ministry from anything other than a sense of joy is to offer to my brother or sister a cold, resentful heart. To be ministers by using the gifts with which we are blessed is authentic discipleship.

This true story illustrates what can happen when one engages in ministry by doing something that gives her or him pleasure. A middle-aged engineer was the first person to join our inner-city congregation in Washington, D.C. As a new mission congregation we were determined to minister to the needs of the neighborhood assigned to us by the mission board of our church. The needs were great: rats in the alley and in the houses of our neighbors, schools with inadequate libraries and music programs, runaway youth with no place to go, young people on drugs, boarding houses filled with lonely people, and many other problems typical of large inner cities.

We were also determined to establish the new congregation with the premise that we discover the gifts and talents of our members and use those gifts in ministry. This was explained as four adults and six children gathered around our dining room table for the first worship service. Let's find out what we enjoy doing, we decided, and see if that will provide a clue to our special gifts. The temptation to assign initial tasks was great because the needs of our neighbors were many.

Several days later our engineer friend, Bob, announced to us that when he came home from his work (which he enjoyed) what he liked doing more than anything else was building model airplanes. The rest of us could hardly keep from laughing. "We're talking about gifts for ministry," we told him. Bob was not to be disuaded. He had a gift for building model airplanes, he insisted, and he thoroughly enjoyed doing it!

During the following week my husband, John, toured the neighborhood, visiting the police station, the fire department, local bars and restaurants, rooming houses, and any place where people gathered. He introduced himself as a new Lutheran pastor in the area and offered the services of the congregation (neglecting to say we had only four members). His last stop was the local playground, where he thanked the director for his care in supervising our children. "Is there anything our congregation can do to assist you?" John asked.

"Not really," the director responded. "Oh, come to think of it, I do have eight boys who need to get ready for a model airplane contest. Do you have anyone who could help them?" Pausing the appropriate amount of time to think, John responded that he was sure he could find someone.

And so it happened that twice a week eight neighborhood boys met in the basement of Bob's house and were taught how to build model airplanes. This was a major step in building up a trust between us and our neighbors. As white "do-gooders" coming into a neighborhood where we were in the minority, we were suspect, to say the least. Bob cared deeply for these boys. When a knife was stolen, the work stopped while a discussion was held on respect for one another's property. In a sense this model-airplane club became the first Christian education class, because the joy and love expressed by Bob witnessed to his faith. Through these boys we met their families and learned not only to know them and their needs, but to share some of the pain and the good times of inner-city living.

As our congregation grew, we discovered different gifts. Val had the gift of hospitality. She announced rather shyly that she enjoyed visiting with people and that the coffee pot would always be on. Val and her husband Bill, who was confined to a wheelchair, had open house day and night. The needs of people came before any work they were doing. Talk and counsel took place over a cup of coffee. Anyone who came, whether friend or someone right off the street, was made to feel welcome and refreshed through this gracious gift of hospitality from two gifted individuals.

Ruth enjoyed working with real estate. She had a unique ability to discover and arrange for the purchase of low-cost houses that we as a congregation would help to renovate. The program she initiated eventually allowed 35 low-income families, who had rented substandard apartments, to become home owners. This ministry would not have happened if Ruth had been assigned a task within the congregation. For two years Ruth continued to ask that someone tell her what she should be doing. She struggled to discover what she enjoyed doing, and finally realized that it was real estate. The result was excitement and fulfillment in her ministry.

Some of us are slow learners. At one time in my life I was certain that I needed to be a junior high teacher because so few teachers seemed willing to struggle with children that age. Fortunately before I took that step I admitted to myself that I was terrified of more than two children that age together in one room. I would have taught with fear and trembling, not with a sense of joy, and the class would have been a disaster. Instead, I became a nurse. It was a way for me to "serve people," I said. When I completed my training, I discovered that as hard as I tried to enjoy nursing, I did not, and as a result was not an especially good nurse.

My brother is a happy, fulfilled man, but he too, struggled to find a life-style that expressed his gifts. Seminary training and parish ministry gave way to law school and the legal profession. Being a lawyer was not satisfying for him either. When he realized "people jobs" were not where his gifts lay, he began to work with his hands. He created wooden toys and designed looms. He learned house construction, plumbing and electrical skills. He and his family are generous people who care about the needs of others. The things my brother *enjoys* doing are the avenues for service that have most benefited others.

To each has been given the manifestation of the Spirit. God's good gifts can be found in each of us.

9

Is Evoking Gifts
a Middle-Class Fad?

It has occurred to me that a book on evoking one another's gifts can be an insult to the majority of people in the world. Does a book like this have meaning only for the middle and upper classes who are supposed to have their lives together? Most of us who are reading this are adequately housed, educated, clothed, and fed, and many of us drive two cars. We have the luxury of reading books on self-fulfillment and attending human-potential classes. We even have the time to discover creativity within ourselves and perhaps add weaving or writing to our list of accomplishments.

If using our gifts puts us in the center of God's will for our lives, what about the millions of people who have no time or energy to use their gifts? For much of the world the necessity of eking out a living leaves no room for evoking another's gift or discovering one's own. For others, using gifts in radical discipleship meets with nothing but failure. Acting within God's will is not a panacea for happiness. These are real-life problems and raise some theological issues.

As we see people caught in unfulfilled, joyless living, we acknowledge our brokenness and our alienation from the One who created us. God's will is not always done. God's will is that we all be whole, but we still see shattered lives. Jesus came to bring peace, but there is still strife. We are meant to be healed and exist in a saving relationship with our Lord, but many are not. The process of sanctification meant to make us whole (holy) is not always evident in our struggle to make sense out of our lives.

Evidence of brokenness does not negate the importance of understanding and using what the Spirit has given us. Perhaps it is when we sense the pain of life most acutely that we need one another to help discover who we really are. The apostle Peter, writing to the early Christians suffering persecution, did not waver in his certainty as to how the oppressed are to live:

> Above all hold unfailing your love for one another, since love covers a multitude of sins. Practice hospitality ungrudgingly to one another. As each has received a gift, employ it for one another, as good stewards of God's varied grace (1 Peter 4:8-10).

These are incredible words, considering the circumstances under which Peter was writing. Even though he felt the end times were near, he was still concerned that Christians expend their Spirit-gifts on one another and love unconditionally.

I would never assume that I know how it is to live as an oppressed person. Therefore, I would not prescribe a life-style for them. Regardless of our circumstances, there is a connection between us. A pastor living on a lake in northern Minnesota attended a conference held in a migrant farm worker camp in Florida. After three days of listening to the problems of these migrant workers, the pastor made an honest observation and confession. "My daily existence in Minnesota is so far from what I am seeing and hearing, I simply cannot relate to the situation. The only thing I can say is I will never take what I have for granted."

This is a good place for us to begin. Appreciating our gifts and being stewards of God's varied grace is the framework within which we are to live. Those of us who see life as gift instead of drudgery, suffering, or struggle, need to remember that our gifts are pure grace. The Spirit gave them for a purpose. Seeing others in need, we put our grace-gifts in perspective and lavishly expend them on others.

10

No Rules but One:
For the Common Good

"There are no rules about leaping into the new because nobody has ever been there before." This maxim decorates my desk. It reminds me that I am free to take risks using my gifts and even free to fail. There is no need to conform to another's opinion of me. There is no one with whom I can be compared, because when I use my talents in their unique combination, I am exploring new space. There is a sense of exhilaration in the knowledge that I am free to leap into the unknown, but at the same time it is unsettling for me. I am more secure keeping my gifts neatly tied up within myself than allowing them to thrust me into the unknown.

No rules, and yet one very important rule: "To each is given the manifestation of the Spirit for the common good" (1 Cor. 12:7).

Here we go again! Just when we are beginning to realize that to use our gifts is to be fully what God intended us to be and that we are to enjoy ourselves using our gifts, the church throws out the same old line with the same old hook. We "ought to" use our gifts for others. The bottom line—the small print—is always the same. We dare not be selfish. It's just a variation of the old theme, it's better to give than to receive. Where is the freedom in being told what I must do with my gift? What about my own fulfillment? Where is the good news?

The good news is that we are most fulfilled when we are using our gift for others. The good news comes when we realize that our life together in Christian community is more satisfying, more joyful, and more creative when there are guidelines and a common discipline. Creativity seldom comes as a result of chaos, but is a result of discipline. Just as children are more creative and sense freedom when some limits are set, so it is with the body of Christ. Through the ages the church has realized the importance of a common understanding of how we care for one another. The rule of St. Benedict, the Rule of Taize, the golden rule—these are examples of how the people of God live together in love and peace. Peter's pastoral advice is in a sense the "rule" by which the healthy, responsible body of Christ is to function. "As each has received a gift, employ it for one another."

Martin Luther wrote, "All we have should be used in service, and whatever is not used in service has been stolen." Luther often emphasized that those who understand their salvation and completely trust God for everything are completely free to serve others. These people no longer live for self but rather completely for the community of saints. "Everyone has been created and born for the sake of the other." The paradox of gospel living is expressed by Luther's words, "A Christian is a perfectly free lord of all, subject to none. A Christian is a perfectly dutiful servant of all, subject to all."

When gifts are used for others, the giver also benefits. The artist who paints and then hides his picture in a closet not only robs others of pleasure, but diminishes his own sense of pleasure. Single friends of mine often say how cheated they feel when they have prepared a delicious meal and have no one with whom they can share it. Friends who keep journals and share their gift of writing through letters, share themselves in a special way.

"Like clouds and wind without rain is a man who boasts of a gift he does not give" (Prov. 25:14). God has made us to feel wholeness when we are giving of ourselves. This is not a law, it is a simple fact, witnessed to by men and women who have discovered that it is in giving they have received. Whether one is a star or a candle, what good is the light if there is no one present to see and share its beauty!

11

The Spirit Knows
Which Gifts Are Needed

It is fortunate none of us must decide which gifts would be appropriate for the common good. We would never begin to guess the many needs of others! But the Spirit knows. This is why the variety is so great and why no gift is to be despised. God's Spirit is capricious and courageous. All of the grace-gifts given in the body of Christ are "inspired by one and the same Spirit, who apportions to each one individually as he wills" (1 Cor. 12:11). Therefore there are not holy and unholy gifts. Those who are tempted to keep score are apt to see some gifts as more appropriate to kingdom-building than others. This is why Paul wanted to make certain we understood that our gifts—the way we serve and all the "varieties of working"—differ, but "to *each* is given the manifestation of the Spirit for the common good."

Because we are graced and gifted by the Spirit of God blowing through us, we must not expect Spirit activity to be static. Many Christians testify that for a period of time, or under a certain set of circumstances, God's Spirit provided them with a gift they did not even realize they possessed. They were surprised, but they should not have been, for we are new every day, always becoming what God wants us to be. When a need arises, gifts are provided. Creation is an ongoing process and includes new stirrings within us. With Martin Luther King Jr., we can say:

We ain't what we oughta be,
We ain't what we wanna be,
We ain't what we gonna be,
But thank God, we ain't what we was!

This does not mean we are given permission to slide again into conditional living, waiting for the "real me" to emerge. We do ourselves a disservice by refusing to accept the reality of who we are and where we now have the opportunity for ministry. We have this one day to be faithful, and we need to live *this* time and celebrate it fully. God's Spirit will continue to fill us when we continue to empty ourselves, just as Jesus emptied himself, taking the form of a servant (Phil. 2:7).

Spirit gifts are not some magical spell given to a few as proof that God loves one individual more than another. Gifts are given in order to fill a need. They are provided for the good of all so the body of Christ may be strengthened.

Jesus used his gift of healing to meet human need, not for the effect of a magic performance. At times he even asked people not to tell others what he had done. When he fed hungry people with bread and fish, he was again meeting human need, not auditioning for a greater-than-thou exhibition. When the scribes and the Pharisees asked Jesus for a sign, he responded that it is an evil and adulterous generation who insists on a sign. As Jonah was in the whale's belly for three days, so the Son of man will be three days in the earth (Matt. 12:38-40). This is the sign of total, self-giving love displayed on a cross. There is no greater gift to give.

The church is haunted by the Holy Ghost. Consider for a moment how pervasive and relentless the Spirit is. God's people need teachers, so teaching gifts are given. When people are tempted to become enculturated and lose their leavening ability, prophetic voices are raised up from among us. Our prophets, as irritating as they may be, remind us again of what it means to be yeast in our society—active bubbles of faithful communities. Some of us are given the gift of discernment, and others are engaged in healing ministries. To enrich prayer life some speak in tongues, while others interpret this prayer language. Paul even lists administrators (far down the list, but who's keeping score!) as a gift to the body (1 Cor. 12).

To the church at Rome Paul writes that our gifts differ according to the grace given us. He assured his readers that some were given the gift of service or the ability to give aid when needed. A Spirit gift that is probably the least exercised is to give generously of your money. Some are able to be persuasive and others to give good advice or warning. It is a Spirit gift to be merciful and give of your time (Rom. 12: 3-8). Paul by no means exhausts the list of spiritual gifts, but his examples give us an idea of the infinite variety.

For any of us to deny we have spiritual gifts is to misunderstand gifts as supernatural magic and not see our gifts as tools for discipleship. They are called spiritual gifts because they are given by the Spirit, not because they somehow have more to do with "heavenly" pursuits than with our "earthiness." It is a Greek concept to divide ourselves into body, mind, and spirit. Our Hebrew heritage presents a picture

80

of wholeness. We are enlivened by the Spirit for ministry here on our earth home. Spirit gifts do not call us away from our humanness but call us into life as we experience it among our sisters and brothers.

At the end of 1 Corinthians 12, Paul could have written to us. "Are all of you apostles? Are all prophets? Do all work in real estate? Are all teachers? Do all build model airplanes? Would all give a hug to a stranger in a laundry room? Do all speak in tongues?" By these rhetorical questions Paul is saying we can trust the Spirit to provide the individuals necessary for a whole, healthy community of saints.

Paul ends 1 Corinthians 12 by writing, "But earnestly desire the higher gifts. And I will show you a still more excellent way." Then he continues with the familiar 13th chapter: "If I speak in the tongues of men and of angels, but have not love, I am a noisy gong or a clanging cymbal." If we cannot say "Jesus is Lord" except by God's Spirit in us, certainly we cannot *love* unless God in us is making this gift visible through us. Love, too, is a gift because love is of God, St. John tells us. Any gift we may possess, if not given to others with the gift of love, is like so much clatter and empty noise. The receiver senses the empty gesture because the gift is given more out of our own need than out of genuine caring for the other.

My friend Jim Smith is an electrician. Recently a letter he wrote made me realize how concrete and important loving can be when we live with a sense of Christian vocation as we exercise our gifts. Jim wrote, "My work must reflect an attitude of caring for the people who hire me and also reflect care of the environment. I cannot forget the consumptive nature of my work, and I try to keep that consumption to a minimum. I value my work—not just its economic value—but its value as a service to others. I keep in mind that my work is not done for machines, but for people. It doesn't matter if I am working for a customer or for a friend, because I do the same quality of work for both. I want to reflect a caring and loving attitude."

Noisy gongs and clanging cymbals call attention to themselves. Gifts given in love call attention to the Christ in us, from whom comes every good and every perfect gift. What a sense of freedom it is to know that God's Spirit is in control, providing the gifts necessary for the common good!

12

With Jesus
Every Day Is Not Nice

I do not want to give the impression that discerning and using our gifts is a sure way to be successful. Our attempts at ministry do not always leave us feeling happy and do not always "work." In human terms not everything "worked" for Jesus. He ended up on a cross.

At a recent pastoral conference John lectured on the theology of the cross. In the afternoon I gave a presentation on evoking gifts. At the conclusion a hand went up. "Why do you two disagree?" I was asked. "This morning we heard the theology of the cross, and this afternoon you gave us theology of glory."

The statement surprised me and I hardly knew how to respond. Theology of glory! The phrase conjured up a variety of theological assumptions that to me are the opposite of self-giving love—assumptions such as hollow optimism, success-oriented Christianity, a heaven-centered vision, and a bumper sticker I had seen that said "With Jesus Every Day Is Nice." Perhaps my illustrations of people using their gifts all had happy endings and seemed too easy. I had failed to mention that our engineer friend who helped the neighborhood boys build model airplanes was reported to the authorities by his white neighbor. An obscure Washington, D.C., ordinance (no more than two persons can be tutored in a private residence) resulted in his arrest. Should I have told about a young friend who was raped twice by those she was trying to help? I thought of Jim and Cheryl, who have struggled for years to effect some change in local and state legislation for minority rights. Although it is with humor they tell their stories of rebuke, failure, and threats, Jim admits that not much of what he does is very successful.

Success isn't the point, and Jim knows it. The point is faithfulness. That's why he keeps using his gifts in a difficult ministry. Jim knows he is called to be faithful to his understanding of how the gospel is to be made visible in his life. Jim and Cheryl do not always live with optimism, but they live with hope. They trust the promises of God as they use their gifts to work for justice and wholeness for all of God's people. This is hope! God does not endow us with gifts and then leave us. Our God is no absentee landlord. The Holy Ghost haunts our house, turning and turning us to insure that we are at least facing in the right direction. With this Spirit activity inhabiting our house, we should not be surprised that our gifts will take us out into the world, and sometimes this will hurt. Reading Mark's gospel, we see that as Jesus taught, he followed his teaching by an image of the suffering servant:

> If any man would come after me, let him deny himself and take up his cross and follow me. For whoever would save his life will lose it, and whoever loses his life for my sake and the gospel's will save it (Mark 8:34-35).

Or again: "And he began to teach them that the Son of man must suffer many things, and be rejected . . . and be killed, and after three days rise again" (Mark

8:31). When Peter began to admonish Jesus for exposing this truth, Jesus harshly said, "Get behind me, Satan! For you are not on the side of God, but of men."

Jesus leaves no doubt that the power of the disciple will be the exact opposite of power as the world defines it:

> You know that those who are supposed to rule over the Gentiles lord it over them, and their great men exercise authority over them. But it shall not be so among you; but whoever would be great among you must be your servant, and whoever would be first among you must be slave of all. For the Son of man also came not to be served but to serve, and to give his life as a ransom for many (Mark 10:42-45).

"Are you able to drink the cup that I drink or to be baptized with the baptism with which I am baptized?" Jesus asks his disciples (Mark 10:38). We may quickly answer as did the disciples, "Yes, we are able." Then we learn, much to our dismay, that we might be called upon to minister where it is messy. To be a follower of The Way, as the early Christians were called, is to live with the possibility that when our gifts are used for the common good, we may find ourselves in a suffering servant role. We may find ourselves on streets that are not safe, in situations that are not secure and comfortable, in homes that are not peaceful and at bedsides of despair. We will probably be tempted to echo the sentiments of the young son of a pastor friend. After six months in a very difficult inner-city parish his comment was, "I know God probably wants us here, daddy, but let's do what we're supposed to do and get out!"

This radical cup we are to drink—could it be social ostracism because of a stance we take for the sake of Jesus? Does the baptism of which Jesus was speaking include ridicule because we use our gifts to do foolish things for him? The world smirks behind our back when we forget self and look first to the needs of others. We will be looked in the eye and called a fool when we use our gift of exhortation to urge others to join us in prayers for our enemies instead of devising new ways to kill them.

John Howard Yoder during a lecture at Holden Village made the comment that we cannot always look down the cross and see a resurrection at the other end. I think this is another way of saying that with Jesus every day is *not* nice. This does not alter our stance of servanthood but helps us understand that the *results* of our strongest efforts lie within the providence of God, not with us. We understand grace in the realm of personal salvation—God's work, not ours—but in the realm of history we forget about grace and conclude that making history come out right is up to us. Our responsibility lies in using our gifts, knowing that not even a cross without a resurrection can separate us from the love of God.

Even on mornings when we are not "up" we can be assured God is present. The God with us is not a smiling, benign grandfather who pats us on the head and says, "Cheer up! Because you love me every day is going to be just great!" I can remember the 5:00 A.M. feeding time for our first baby. Having been up much of the night, I was half awake as I would fumble with a wet diaper, heat up a bottle, and sink into the chair in front of the television set to feed our screaming child. With my toe I would push the *on* button of the T.V. and was always greeted by a man with a large set of white teeth. He would smile at me from the screen and croon, "Good morning. Isn't it a lovely day? Look at me. I'm smiling." The camera would zoom in for a close-up of Mr. Teeth. "I haven't even had a cup of coffee, but I'm smiling because Jesus loves me!"

We don't have to pretend each day is beautiful. The God who is present with us in our brokenness and alienation understands suffering, regardless of the reason for it. God promises to be with us in our failures, because it is in the depths of frustration and despair that we most clearly recognize our need for a gracious God.

Hope for many of us is that fragile stem connecting our roots in the promises of God with the tiny bud of faithful living that sometimes flowers and sometimes does not. Hope is knowing that our present feeling of failure is not permanent and that God has the last word. Hope is not much to go on, but it is enough. Because of hope we are free to risk being servants—willing servants, suffering servants—understanding we are people of the cross.

Our cross is like our Lord's—

The end of a path freely chosen after counting the cost—

The price of our social nonconformity—

The social reality of representing the order to come in an unwilling world (John Howard Yoder in *Politics of Jesus*).

13

The Joy of
Risking Our Gifts

In Margery Williams' book, the *Velveteen Rabbit*, a toy rabbit and a skin horse are talking as they lie side by side in the nursery. Their conversation goes like this:

"What is REAL?" asked the Rabbit one day, when they were lying side by side. . . . "Does it mean having things that buzz inside you and a stick-out handle?"

"Real isn't how you're made," said the Skin Horse. "It's a thing that happens to you. When a child loves you for a long, long time, not just to play with, but REALLY loves you, then you become Real."

"Does it hurt?" asked the Rabbit.

"Sometimes," said the Skin Horse, for he was always truthful. "When you are Real you don't mind being hurt."

"Does it happen all at once, like being wound up," he asked, "or bit by bit?"

"It doesn't happen all at once," said the Skin Horse. "You become. It takes a long time. That's why it doesn't often happen to people who break easily, or have sharp edges, or who have to be carefully kept. Generally, by the time you are Real, most of your hair has been loved off, and your eyes drop out and you get loose in the joints and very shabby. But these things don't matter at all, because once you are Real you can't be ugly, except to people who don't understand."

In our fantasy we may hold a dream of being that beloved, shabby skin horse. The joy of the toy was that he had given himself to another for so long he finally became real. Real. Human. Humans are made for loving others. This is why we laugh and cry so easily together. It is the result of placing ourselves within God's will for our lives, because his will is that we be fully who we are—creatures capable of deep love.

Each of us experiences times in our lives when we are overcome by love for another. At these times it is easy to understand the kind of self-giving love of the suffering servant. We would have given our life if that were required of us, because the love we had completely took over concern for self. Egoism had been smothered.

The problem is that there are too few times of sustained love for others in our lives. Our circle of loving, if there at all, is quite small. The radical lover is one who has tasted the joy promised in doing servant acts and has loved his or her way into a servant's mind. With a servant's mind, loving comes easily. When we are tempted to withhold our gift because it may cause us pain or inconvenience, we have the example of the one we call Lord. Having prayed in all honesty, pleading with his father to find another way, Jesus, who for the joy that was set before him, endured the cross, despising the shame (Heb. 12:2).

There is joy in risking. Joy comes with the assurance that God is in control just as in the past, and will continue to be in the future. The reason we are able to use our gifts for one another—and perhaps to suffer ridicule, loss of material goods or time, physical or mental abuse—is because the Spirit who gives us the gifts also gives us the grace and strength to employ them. This is the good news. We are not left with a set of do-it-yourself instructions, but with the promises of God's presence and power, if only we are willing to risk sharing what has been given to us.

Our fear of risk and perhaps failure keeps many of us in our playpens. We are fearful of using a gift and looking foolish in our weakness. In a community of Christians we can celebrate together our individual and corporate weakness. This is where we remind one another that God's power is made perfect in our weakness (2 Cor. 12:9). If we could do everything right, everything by ourselves there would be no need for God. Celebrate our weakness, as hard as that is! Weakness and dependence on God is the opposite of having security in neat-answer packages where everything is tied up for us in pink ribbon. We may discover our weakness when we leap out into the unknown, turned upside down and inside out by the Spirit catching our unfurled heart. But here is where we discover our strength—God's strength.

James Carroll speaks to the joy of risk in his poem from *Elements of Hope*. Peter and the disciples are in a fishing boat.

> "Isn't that him
> walking on the water?"

Oh, Peter, please, no more
of your foolishness.
What we need in times
like these of crisis
are restraint and common sense.
"No, no. Just look! There!
Don't you see the figure there
where the waves crest.
I'd swear it's him."
Peter, stop and think.
Water will support no one.
Men sink. Besides
He is gone. We must live
without visions. Without him.
"But I tell you
it is *him!*
He is beckoning."
Peter, we worry about
you. You are not yourself.
You were a practical man.
We hate to say it, but
you may need professional help.
"Stand back!
I'm going over."
We cannot permit it.
You will drown.
You are not responsible.
"Let go of me!
It's *him.* He's calling me!"
Peter, we hate to
use force. Quit struggling.
The water will not hold you.
It would not hold him
even if he were here.

But he is gone!
He would want you
to be sensible.
Think, Peter, think!
"Give me my cloak!"
That's more foolishness of yours.
No one *puts on* a cloak
before jumping in the water.
"Give it to me!
He is waiting!"
Well, can you swim?
Oh, dear. He's gone.
Swim, Peter, swim!
Do you see that?
Do you see that?
Why, good old Peter
is walking on the water!
And look, do you see?
What do you think of that?
I think Peter is magnificent
in his backwardness;
We might towel ourselves
before bathing or say
good-bye on meeting.
But Peter! He wraps himself
in death before
leaping into life.

Peter's action was very different from the action of
the third servant in the parable of the talents. The
third servant did not realize he was free to fail, and
that if he did fail, God would be there to pick up the
pieces. When we are afraid to risk what has been

given to us, we are like the servant who carefully wrapped his talent in a clean handkerchief and hid it in the ground only to discover that later it is taken away from him and given to someone more responsible. By his fearful action he was unable to enter into the joy of the master. The risks may sometimes be great, but when we reach out to another, overcome by love, we find ourselves surprised by joy.

14

The Common Good Is
Larger Than We Thought

In Chapter 10 we discussed the use of our gifts for the common good. But how far does common good extend? Are gifts to be used primarily for our immediate family?

God bless me and my wife,
Our Bill and his wife,
Us four, no more. Amen

Are they used only for our neighbors—just as long as they are polite, clean and grateful? You know, *our* kind of people.

For our church—the saints but not the sinners?

For our country—as long as it remains democratic, capitalistic, and calls itself Christian?

We learned something about the size and condition of our family one Thanksgiving day in Washington, D.C. Our small congregation decided to invite all those in our parish area to share Thanksgiving dinner with us. Each family prepared a turkey dinner, complete with appetizer and dessert. We set up tables in the basement of a nearby Presbyterian church and decorated them with linen tablecloths, flowers, and our best dishes and silverware. Our family brought along our traditional pilgrim and turkey candles—the kind you bring out every year for decoration but never let the kids light.

The week before Thanksgiving, we posted mimeographed invitations throughout the neighborhood: "Anyone who is alone, has no place to go or who wants to share Thanksgiving with others, is invited to dinner at . . . ." We listed the time and place, and the children decorated the signs. On Thursday each family assembled around their table in the church basement and waited to see who would come.

The variety was typical of the racial and economic mix of our neighborhood. At our table was a mother on welfare with her two young children and a teen-ager spaced out on drugs. One of our guests was an inebriated man we had often seen slumped in our alley nursing his bottle of Thunderbird. He imme-diately set about lighting our collection of pilgrim and turkey candles, as our youngest daughter wailed loudly. There was a runaway girl and a foreign stu-dent from a nearby rooming house. As we looked around the room, the variety was repeated at every table. It didn't take long for the awkward silence to give way to the gentle hum of normal table conver-sation. When the day was over, none of the thanks for the food and hospitality could come close to the sense of gratitude our family felt for being part of a much larger family. It was not only gratitude we felt, but also a new awareness that as Christians we are called to share the humanity of the whole fam-ily of God.

Our ring of love widens as we study God's Word. Scripture gives ample evidence that our gifts are not only given to strengthen the church, but if we are to follow Jesus, the gifts are to be used in ministry in the world. These two areas of our concern are not mutually exclusive. They are inseparable if we are to be disciples. The body of Christ is made strong in order to be a working organism, fit for servant acts in society. The social importance of using gifts creatively is evident because in society the result of unfulfillment and lack of creative expression is often manifested in violence. Dr. Kurt Adler writes, "More and more individuals are coming to feel they are nonpersons. . . . From this comes a feeling of insignificance. Violence is a way of proving that one exists, when one believes oneself to be insignificant."

Violence is essentially a form of noncreative communication. E. F. Schumacher in *Good Work* says, "When one is deprived of the power of expression or creativity, one will express him or herself in a drive for violence." Much violence is the result of impotence stemming from our failure to help our sisters and brothers discover their uniqueness.

Living for eight years in Washington, D.C., during the struggle of blacks for civil rights, we were aware of this truth as we watched our city being torn apart by violence. Eric, an eight-year-old black child, was an example of someone who felt he was nonperson. Eric was part of an after-school tutoring program our congregation initiated. He was in the second grade and read very poorly. When we realized that most of the books we had collected showed only white children, we made an attempt to secure children's literature showing black people and other minorities. We eagerly waited for Eric's response as he paged through the new books. His reaction was unexpected, but it should not have been. As he saw the black children in the pictures, he slammed the book shut and said,

"I don't like this book. Those kids dumb!" At age eight, Eric already had been programmed to believe that white was smart and black was dumb. A violence had been done to Eric in his early years, as it had been done to his teenaged brother and sisters and to his parents.

The world is full of Erics and their families who feel impotent and frustrated. The migrant worker, the abandoned old man, the overworked and the underpaid, the abused spouse, the prisoner, the ridiculed child—these and many more have no outlet through which they can creatively express their rage at being treated as subhuman. When creativity is stifled, hostility increases. Eric, too, is a gifted human being, but he had never been told this. He needed to be given a chance to express his uniqueness in a creative way. Eric is part of our much larger common family, and our gifts need to be directed toward helping him discover who he is. To show compassion one cannot be paternalistic, but must begin to break down the many walls of hostility we have allowed to separate us from other family members.

15

An Even Wider *Shalom* Claims Our Gifts

Robert Frost wrote:

Something there is that doesn't love a wall,
That sends the frozen-ground-swell under it,
And spills the upper boulders in the sun;
And makes gaps even two can pass abreast.

While we keep building walls, something there is
that wants to break them down. Jesus gave his life to
break down walls that divide us, and God's Spirit
continues to work through us to "make the gaps
where two can pass abreast."

Wall building can be a subtle process. We find
walls of hostility surrounding us, and we are scarce-
ly aware of how they came to be. One day we realize
we are not communicating with our marriage partner
or find ourselves alienated from our children. We are
angry with family, friends, employer, colleagues. In
our nation we separate ourselves from ghettos, reser-
vations, nursing homes, ethnic groups, and those
whose skin color differs from ours. We drive on four
superlanes edged with crown vetch to keep America
beautiful, and never see the areas of poverty that
exist two miles off the highway.

Our walls are many, and they are strong and high.
They were not built overnight, but stone by stone, as
we exaggerated our differences instead of celebrating
our similarities.

But something there is that doesn't love a wall.
Nature doesn't, Robert Frost tells us. Jesus didn't;
that's why he came, to break down walls of hostility
(Eph. 2:13-18). God continues to work in us and

through us, to break down walls that make us prisoners of our small minds, our prejudices, and our fears. Later in his poem "Mending Wall" Frost says,

> Before I built a wall I'd ask to know
> What I was walling in or walling out,
> And to whom I was like to give offense.
> Something there is that doesn't love a wall,
> That wants it down.

To whom are we likely to give offense? We find ourselves in a world where many we do not even know are offended by us. We need to be reconciled to our global family. Recall the words of Jesus in Matthew 5:23-24: "If you are offering your gift at the altar, and there remember that your brother has something against you, leave your gift there before the altar and go; first be reconciled to your brother." We have tended to view these words as individualistic and concerned only with personal ethics. But our Bible is a Hebrew book. The Hebrew concept of *shalom* is communal and social in nature and knows no boundaries.

We find ourselves part of a system of economics and political strategy that is directly related to the suffering of many people. The greed of wealthy nations creates distribution and trade policies favorable to rich countries. We use land and natural resources from developing nations for our benefit and use food-aid as a weapon. As we go to the altar, do we remember that we are supporting governments in Latin America, Africa, and Asia that oppress the peasants and the have-nots? We should not go to the altar with our gift—a gift perhaps given out of our surplus—and forget those who have no surplus and only the barest means of sustenance. Jesus was not telling us to go out and be reconciled because he wanted us to feel guilty. He is talking about remembering—remembering our brother and sister. He is setting priorities straight. We ought not tell God of our love without loving in word and in deed those for whom Jesus died.

Even when we understand how wide the circle of *shalom* needs to extend, we are at a loss as to how to use our gifts to carry out the ministry of reconciliation. Maybe stars can shed light on some of these wider needs, but as candles we feel we'd be snuffed out in no time. The wind outside our family circle is just too strong! Besides, acknowledging oneself to be a "have" in a world of "have-nots" is to admit that we have benefited in many ways from the system that helped create this worldwide gap. We don't want to live with less and at the same time feel guilty and impotent to change what we do not like about this system of inequality.

We know many of our global family "have something against us," but the principalities and powers that control our lives overwhelm us and we feel little or no control over our circumstances. How can we begin to use our gifts for these global concerns?

Many struggle with a response of discipleship. Distinguished lay theologian and lawyer, Jacques Ellul says, "I always apply a motto: 'Think globally, act locally.' . . . . By thinking globally I can analyze all the phenomena, but when it comes to acting, it can only be local . . . . if it is to be honest, realistic and authentic."

Think globally, act locally. This is also the advice given by Latin American liberation theologian, José Miguez-Bonino. Our daughter, while helping to host Miguez-Bonino on her university campus, expressed to him her frustration at being unable to find concrete ways in which to participate in reconciliation between the United States and nations of the third and fourth worlds. "What can a concerned Christian do? Do more of us need to go to your country and work among the people? Do we send agronomists, technicians, teachers, or pastors?" Karen asked him.

Act locally, was the essence of the theologian's answer. "Stay where you are. Speak with those in your own country about their life-styles. Help your own people to see that the way of life espoused by many in the wealthy nations of the world is part of the problem."

Later, as he spoke informally with students, one agitated young woman exploded with, "But sir, don't we first have to find Jesus for ourselves before we can minister to the poor and the oppressed?"

We all need to hear his answer. "In your brother and sister is where you *will* find Jesus," he said.

The prophet Jeremiah proclaimed that to know Yahweh is to do justice. Jesus lays before us the same priority when he tells us to first seek the kingdom of God and his justice. Doing justice requires the many gifts found within the body of Christ. The gifts of faith and the gifts of love enable us to see things differently. "It is not so much the way we grab things as the way we see things," Bishop John Taylor reminds us. When we see injustices, we will respond with our gifts and with our lives. When we see God's bounty as a gift to all people, we will change the way we live. We will step out of engrained patterns of consumption and allow a more just system of distribution to emerge. We show concern globally and act locally by using our Christian citizenship to speak out and to write letters to those in authority, encouraging them to enact just laws.

We also show authentic discipleship when we care for our family, those in our neighborhoods and communities, and all those hidden Americans in rooming houses, mental hospitals, and mountain hollows. This is a realistic approach because it takes the generalization out of our concern and calls upon us to use our gifts for specific individuals in specific situations. It calls us to compassion and creativity.

First be reconciled to your brother and then come and offer your gift. What we offer our brother and sister is a gift of love. As we do this we simultaneously give that gift to God. Paul writes in Romans that we are to owe no one anything but to love them. When we make that love tangible, we witness to the vision of a wide, inclusive *shalom*.

16

The Earth and *Shalom*

Seeing connections not only between us and the rest of humanity, but between us and the created universe leads to a still wider understanding of the common good. *Shalom* (wholeness) as a vision includes our relationship to nature.

"For in him [Jesus] all the fulness of God was pleased to dwell, and through him to reconcile to himself all things, whether on earth or in heaven, making peace by the blood of his cross" (Col. 1:19-20). Not only are *we* reconciled to God, but the cross signalled reconciliation of *everything* in creation. Nature, too, groans, having fallen under generations of humankind who have not always cared for the environment. Wendell Berry, quoted in *Earthkeeping,* says, "A protest meeting on environmental abuse is a convocation of the guilty."

The Christian church, in its preoccupation with personal salvation, has not always been aware of the cosmic dimensions of God's act of reconciliation. In our own country the Puritans were among the first to look upon the forces of nature as something to be controlled, manipulated, and spent. The mentality of the Western frontier was to conquer and control the environment. Axes were not gentle, and no one except the native Americans were calling the earth "mother" or speaking of the animals as our "brothers." Chief Seattle's prophecy may yet be fulfilled: "The whites too shall pass; perhaps sooner than all other tribes. Continue to contaminate your bed, and you will one night suffocate in your own waste."

A Wintu Indian observed that wherever white

man has touched the earth it is sore. Sore earth. Sore animals, with whom we shared a day in Genesis creation history, hunted to extinction. Sore fields as each year topsoil lost from our farms disappears at the rate of twelve tons per acre. Adam was told to till *(abad)* and keep *(shamar)* the land. These Hebrew words mean to serve and to watch over and preserve. To understand humankind as part of the creation, and not superior to it, is the first step in witnessing to the message that God's reconciling act on the cross meant *shalom* for everything God had made.

As we begin the decade of the 1980s, our gifts need to focus on care of our earth home. Farmers who tenderly care for the land, considering its future use rather than immediate profit, are being reconcilers. When we create compost so that our garbage is returned to the earth, we are performing a *shalom* act. The company president who refuses to dump raw industrial wastes into the river conveniently running near the plant, is living in God's *shalom*. Parents who teach their children to enjoy nature without destroying it, convey to those children the message of reconciliation. Everyone who understands how poor our life would be without animals, fish and clear streams, and who encourages others to live with this understanding, is using a gift to share the *shalom* vision.

We are caretakers, earthkeepers, stewards, as well as part of the substance of the creation. Walls dividing us from the rest of creation fall when we can sing with St. Francis:

Praised be my Lord for our sister the moon and the
stars.

Praised be my Lord for our brother the wind and for
air.

Praised be my Lord for our sister the water, and our
brother the fire.

Praised be my Lord for our mother earth, who nour-
ishes and governs us.

Praise, bless and thank my Lord, and serve him with
great humility.

God reminds us we are tenants living with a use
permit on land that is not ours. "Behold, to the Lord
your God belong heaven and the heaven of heavens,
the earth with all that is in it" (Deut. 10:14). "The
land is mine; you are strangers and sojourners with
me" (Lev. 25:23). To see the earth as "borrowed from
our children instead of inherited from our fathers,"
is to live with a *shalom* vision. Our gifts are also given
for the good of the world we share with the rest of
creation. We must tenderly caress it.

17

Equipping the Saints

Evening forums at Holden Village take place around a central fireplace in a building we call Koinonia. *Koinonia* is the Greek word for *fellowship*, yet neither the name nor the symbolic circle of people prevents heated exchange between those with differing viewpoints. One such "white knuckle session" took place this week as the community discussed the role of clergy and lay people. A layman picked up a Bible and banged on it with his fist. "According to Ephesians 4, my pastor should be equipping me for ministry. This is not being done in my congregation. The pastor does everything himself. I have no sense of responsibility for the life of my parish, and I don't know how to minister outside the church walls."

One clergyman, trying not to sound too defensive, quickly answered. "When I try to give my people responsibility, they won't accept it. I feel like a kept-woman or hired help that is to do ministry for them." The discussion continued on into the evening. It was evident that after centuries of clergy-dominated ministry, the authority of ordained clergy and the emerging role of laity were misunderstood and headed on a collision course.

The church will never be a vital, lively, life-changing fellowship if we allow or expect our pastors to be the only ministers. Each of us is a minister. The status of clergy differs from that of laity only as to function. "And his gifts were that some should be apostles, some prophets, some evangelists, some pastors and teachers for the equipment of the

116

saints for the work of ministry, for building up the body of Christ" (Eph. 4:11-12). The pastoral role is to equip those of us within the body for *our* ministry, not to do the ministry for us. There is a vast, untapped source of ministry within lay people.

This is such an important concept to understand, and yet I have not heard of a seminary course called "How to Equip the Saints," or "The Necessity of Evoking Gifts." Our pastors are taught biblical exegesis and systematic theology. They are trained to teach, preach, and counsel, and have some understanding of church history. Seldom in any discussion of models for ministry is there emphasis on discovering and using the gifts of the people of God— not just within the church, but in the world. Pastors who do not see each person under their care as having unique potential for mission and ministry will spend very little time equipping that person for gift-giving.

To equip means to provide the tools necessary for discipleship in a world that is alien to many of our Christian values. Saints are equipped when they are nurtured in the Word and sacraments. We need to be encouraged to ask the hard faith questions, not given easy doctrinal answers. When we meet with others in small mission/ministry groups to help each other discover and use our Spirit gifts, we give and are given tools for discipleship. We can expect to be prayed for, just as we engage in the discipline of prayer for the other members of the body.

Some congregations do realize that ministry is to

be shared. Sunday bulletins are called "staff notes," and the people are informed of when the "ministers" meet throughout the week to be equipped for servanthood. More pastors now feel free to call on members to assist in responding to needs that once were seen as the exclusive area of clergy concern. Pastors who equip the saints tell us they feel less jealous of the role of laity as coministers and also less guilty that they are somehow shirking their responsibilities when they share a ministry.

When we invite a pastor to share our life, we set that person aside for specific equipping duties. We want the pastor free of financial burdens so she or he can do some full time dreaming for the congregation. We want to be challenged by the Word of God and helped to have our gifts evoked. The pastor is the one who makes sure that no one within the body is overlooked or falls between the cracks of structure and programs. Though the pastor may have the responsibility for the larger view of mission and ministry, even this is shared by all the members of the body of Christ.

There is an assumption being made, of course, that the laity willingly accept their role as coministers. The universal priesthood of all believers is intricately woven into the fabric of the Reformation but it always needs to be made specific. We cannot expect our pastors to be everything to everybody. This is why we have a shared priesthood. "You are a chosen race, a royal priesthood, a holy nation, God's own people"

(1 Peter 2:9). Our pastor is no more and no less gifted than any of us in the body of Christ.

We are equipped for life not only within the church, but for our life in the world. The way we are a friend to another, the way we are compassionate and show mercy, the way we relate to our children, write a letter, treat an employee, or wait on a customer—all of these are part of our vocation as people of God confronted by the gospel. In a paper for the American Lutheran Church on the role of laity Beulah Laursen speaks to the issue of lay mission:

> Relevant theology has less to do with watching for opportunities for evangelism than with the way one performs one's daily tasks. It has less to do with having prayer with a client than in serving that client in a just and productive way. It has much to do with the Christian dimension of on-the-job behavior; with the moral and ethical decisions of any trade or profession; with the way one sees oneself in relation to God, neighbor, nature, and the structures of society. It is a theology of responsibility accompanied by a theology of grace which forgives and sustains the erring one when wrong choices are made.

A theology of responsibility accompanied by a theology of grace. This phrase should be written on our walls or worn as frontlets above our eyes, for it is the banner of Christian discipleship. With clergy and laity responsibly exercising their gifts, the transforming power of God's spirit will revitalize the church in ways never before imagined! Tongues of fire will dance on our heads, bringing light to our nearly darkened world.

18

The Shape of Our Gift
Is the Shape of the Cross

Many books are never really completed. They are concluded only by the response of the reader. Because you are reading and not visiting with me you cannot ask me questions. You cannot engage me in debate as a friend of mine does who read my manuscript. He wonders if people who honestly do not feel gifted will be helped or intimidated by what I have written. My distinction of candle and star gifts implies a judgment, he says. He keeps asking me to clarify the relationship between following Jesus and using our gifts.

Recently in a sermon our pastor, Joel, helped clarify this relationship. "The shape of our gift is the shape of the cross," he said. "To pick up our gift is to pick up the cross." Compassionate use of our grace-gifts for others reflects the cross—symbol of giving ourselves away. We follow the example of Jesus, who used his gifts in self-giving love. Exercising our gifts is how we live out our understanding of what it means to be people of the cross. In other words, commitment to our Lord is not walking down a sawdust trail in a revival tent or any other emotional religious experience, but discipleship at the point of using our gifts for others.

My friend also keeps asking me if it is important to know we are gifted. I can only answer him that we do suffer when we feel unfulfilled and sense no "call" upon our lives. To be whole people we must recognize our uniqueness. Fulfilled people are those who are living up to their potential. *Apart* from the body of Christ we may feel incomplete, but as a part of the

122

body it is easier to understand how our particular gift is needed to help make God's people whole.

Gordon Cosby, in a sermon at the Church of the Savior, told his congregation, "Christ makes each of us something unlike any other creation ever fashioned by God—something wonderful, exciting, unique, and something strangely needed in the total body of Christ. This uniqueness, this very self which is so hard to describe, this charismatic person, is the gift of the Holy Spirit. It is the primary gift that we bring to the Body, and without it the Body is immeasurably impoverished." Corporate and individual impoverishment is the result of our failing to evoke and to affirm the gifts of one another.

My friend Anne is the postmistress of a small rural town. Much of the life of this farming community centers around the activity in the tiny brick building that serves as the post office. As I sat there one morning sharing a thermos of coffee with her, I was aware that she counsels, listens carefully, personally delivers mail to neighbors who are ill and befriends those whom the local gossip would malign. Her home has always been a place of open hospitality. Anne tells me she has been keeping up correspondence with a young teenage mother who used to live next to the post office. The young woman never finished high school, but Anne encourages her in her attempts to write poetry and to educate herself. Anne is a gifted woman who cares deeply for others, and yet she told me some days she has the feeling she is wasting her life. "Oh, it's not that I don't recognize I have a gift or two. I just don't feel very talented or feel that what I do each day is very worthwhile," she said.

Anne's sense of fulfillment and living out God's will for her life will depend upon her view, not so much of what she is doing, but of who she is. To live a solitary life, seeing ourselves in isolation from others, is to risk falling into despair. We may try to be all things to all people, compare ourselves to those we consider more gifted, or even develop a "uniquer than thou" attitude. When we see ourselves as part of a whole, as a member of a larger body, we are able to understand the grace and the privilege of participating in a *shalom* community.

Anne would never articulate what we have called the theology of the cross, but she is an example of someone who lives out this theology. She has picked up her gift, her cross, and is using it for others. Like Anne, each of us needs the assurance that we are responding to God's love and celebrating life as we exercise our unique combination of Spirit gifts wherever we find ourselves. We love with a cruciform love. This is the shape of our gift. This is our vocation, our fulfillment, our life.